Musings of Love

Poetic Verse

Musings of Love

Poetic Verse

By Patricia Fointno

KMC Publishing Company, Inc

All Praises to the Head of the Universe
for All Things!

It is with a profound debt of gratitude that I thank the Almighty…the Ancient One, my Mother Cherrie who was on this Earth 104 years.

I would also like to thank my Father Daniel and my Sister Jackie, who also are among the ancestors.

I draw daily inspiration from my daughter, Erin, and my two darling Grands, Christian, and Kaylie.

A very special thanks to Aamir who pushed and focused me to write in the first place.

Thank you for reading

Patricia Fointno

Forethought

Musings

Forethought

Musings of Love is an anthological poetic mantra for lovers. Sight, emotion, and experience are tools that enable the reader to witness, explore and be one with their emotions.

As you read the poems, see how the words vividly conjure up images of that which is in your head and heart. There is something unexplainable about love that takes on the magical and the mystical. The love at work in these poems will take you to a level that sinks in your bones and fills your head and spirit. It will throb in your ears and cast its spell.

The voice you hear is the voice of blackberries and cream all rolled into one. It's raw emotion coming from the heart. This book is for the ceaseless love that is in each one of us. I could no longer ignore mine. When the heat is on, I sweat beads of love that drip down the crevices of my minds' eye into thought pools.

I've Got the Power

I've got the power, yes I do
To make hearts turn and mine too.
Listen to me and you will hear
Whatever your imagination holds, have no fear.

My words are glib, but never glum
And powerful are they
So won't you come?
While I weave the web
And make you think
Of the power I've got
The power to sink
Your heart in mine
And back again.

'Cause the powers' in the word,
And that's fine.
Fine for me and fine for you
All I want is your mind and heart too!

Propositon

I want you under my spell.
How can I persuade you to come into my lair?
I can satisfy the wants and desires of your
innermost passion.

Come On Back In

Come on back in to whatever you want
It's warm, back in to whatever you need
And you need not be afraid,
cause it's warm in here

And I'll be sitting, asking you to do me a favor
And allow yourself to be in, too.
Into what? Into me!

So, come on back in.
Feel the needs of flesh and spirit
Longing to be in…to be into you.
To operate as if one.

To develop a rhythm of passion.
To be obsessed within….possessed within.
So come on back in. Into what? Into me!

Hearing the Call

Thanks for inviting me into your world
A world of glitter and gold and you
My sights are sensing the inevitable 'cause I know
that sooner or later.If you don't back off,
I'll enter your world.

I have already glimpsed your lithe body As you
recline on the bed of Tranquility
To nudge me to cover you with myself
Swelling to the moment of the occasion
Then resting for more.

As I meandered to one side of the arena,
I sensed your presence and knew that
I had woven the initial thread of the web
To back off – and watch you continue weaving.
I shall, but fondly, remember this time,

For actual moments are no more than
Anticipated moments.
Thoughts are so powerful that

I know command levels can captivate
If one has the power
And I have the power to command what I want
And in so commanding
I know that I want you!
So, thanks for understanding
And hearing the call.

The Hunt

You've released an animal and
the game has begun.
The animal that stayed caged for so long
was one who purred and released itself
To satisfy the wants and desires
of innermost passions.

You've released the animal and
now it sniffs your scent.
And anticipates your moves.
And craves those ecstatic desires
Which creep into your psyche and
race to your loins.

You saw the embryonic stage of the animal
and tapped into the long-caged feelings.
To allow me to let go of inhibitions – of the status
quo. To free the spirit – to reach for and
attain the heights which you explore.
And know existed in me.

I'm that animal who desires to
and longs for the hunt – the pursuit
The contact – the capture!
You'd better practice the sport, cause this animal
Is ready to play.

It's in the Plan

Methods of transactions operate in different
modes for different people. Ours has been
calculated to the span of years. Based on voicing
those calculations, we realized that however cool
our exteriors, our interiors are crying with loud
voices to be joined.

Schedules had to be altered, but that was in the
plan. I was way-laid for about an hour and that
was also in the plan. You finally caught my hints,
however subterfuged they were by
this cool exterior.

Our joining last night can only be capsulated into
one word – 'wow'. And, because of time spent
being cool, it makes one wonder if coolness is a
way one is supposed to be.
I knew you'd be waiting for me.

So of course, when I got there it was no surprise
to have you graciously come into my space –
cause that was the way it was supposed to be.
I know all I need to know about you.
Anything of substance, you will reveal to me.
And that is the way it is supposed to be.

Now, the ball game is in your hands, and you carry the bat. So, whenever you think of how revealing I was last night, particularly in how I felt so very comfortable sharing a newly discovered side of me. Know that this was revealed because I knew it was time.

Spans of time are only means to ends. In other words, the distance that separates us can be easily removed so that you will allow me to get into your head and by such removal you'll know that I am ready to share with you what's going on in my head. I know this re-meeting is going to be wonderful. I can't wait for the next.

Predestiny

What a wonderful chance meeting it was, and oh, the sweet rapture of memories treasured in my heart for one Friday, or early Saturday…when two paths already predestined to cross, finally struck that medium of crossing. Spiritually those paths had already met, because there are no chances.

The passion of "I don't know" met with "but you must" and "I don't know said": "Well, who cares…I might not get this chance again for another thousand years, so while it's here, I'll make my move. And if, by chance this medium never comes again I'll bask in the warmth of a smile…a touch…a fleeting cling to caring,"

My heart was filled with the overflow of finally realizing….Oops! It's happening again…those surges of ecstasy that lay dormant…thinking they would never re-surface…but re-surface they did, and refreshing moments they were.

Hard and heavy contemplating followed. Walking and working. Resting and meditating on you! The joy of it all makes for a powerful reflection. Glad you're not here in body, 'cause if you were, until certain hungers had been thoroughly satiated, all zeal would be focused on one endeavor – to get mine – whatever time it took – casting the world to take care of itself for a while, while we toyed with the Kama Sutra and explored on variations of same.

You knew I knew who you were when you called. You volleyed my mind right back into that Friday or early Saturday, and then gently shook me to a future time of tasting sweet nectar from the grapes of ecstasy…of casting cares to winds of forgetfulness…of a further consummation of crossing paths and longings of limbs to intertwine and travel together to the center of the universe…several times!

A cataclysmic meeting I would describe as ours.
And…lest I faint on my feet,
I must not imagine the next!!

Inspiration

I was walking this morning among the stars

And I saw one shining
        – an oracle walking around,
             looking toward me.

I stopped and paused to catch an ear

To hear what he was saying…

I tried to capture the words with each

stroke of my pen

And then I finally realized that

This shining star was YOU.

Thanks

Transcending distance you come to me and I, in turn, drink of thee. The world appears to be a better place – it's a happier time. And I, so engrossed in this total razing of the window, allow airs to permeate the plane, wherein those airs had not been allowed for a long, long time.

Verbal mediums do not catch me by choice and comfort levels are reached expressing thoughts on paper. Maybe because of this mortal spirits' seeking a level of immense immortality – the epitome being caste in stone by these etchings on paper to be read again by this spirit some thousand years from now to remember again that you came to me, once more, when I was ready to receive.

This euphoric state comes easy with you. As I release myself to soaring heights, this freedom feels good, but such loftiness isn't good for the head especially when things appear to be happening on the ground and I'm not there to share with compatriots.

But, who's to care! Endeavors of loftier heights
compel me to 'check them out'. And if, by
chance, you happen to walk with me in heavens
only known to us. And if, by chance, you don't, I
must resign myself to this higher realm 'cause
although dizzingly it takes me, I enjoy this state.

You must know that I am eternally grateful to you
for this revelation. For who's to say that such a
state might have ever been
if our paths had never crossed.

You've Got It

Whatever it is, you've got it. The beat, the style,
for making it. You know the things of time and
space to do it with such flair and grace.
Whatever it is, you've got it.

You had it all the while, you know.
You discovered it long time ago
when you were in your mother's womb,
you waited just to do it – you knew it.

You walk into a room with grace and dazzle all
around the place. They come and bow at your
feet. Your smile they long for to be complete.
Yes, whatever it is, you've got it.

And then you came into my life. One Friday eve
and 'oh' so nice. You dazzled me with charm and
grace and took my heart around the place. Oh,
whatever it is, you've got it.

Don't change a thing just be yourself. And melt
my heart, because it's worth all the noise to be
complete with your soul-mate at your feet.
'Cause whatever it is, you've got it.

I Willed My Soul

I willed my soul to go a while where
you were, and with a smile

My soul took flight and rested there upon
your breast with oh such flair.

Soul went tripping by your face and
saw a smile as on it raced

To capture what it wished to see and
reach into the rest of thee.

I willed my soul to see your heart a ticking
with a brand new start,
And I, I wished to rest a while within
the heart that made me smile.

I willed my soul to follow you,
to see it was, what you do

My soul enveloped you with grace,
and followed you around the place

Soul, it saw a person who, compassion
and caring, he knew.

You are Fantastic

I know that you are in my psyche. You're there
and that's where you know you would be. You
crept in so secretly and worked your way into my
heart. You knew exactly what you were doing
when you sat, and talked and shared our deepest
secrets of time…when we danced and
shared on another level.

I wanted so to have you say: 'lets go and do what
we both know we want to do.' I know that the
levels of understanding are of such that we can
share totally on all three planes – that of the
mental, spiritual and the physical. I believe that
the other planes are going to be heightened
by this kind of communing.

I am short of breath as I anticipate the union.
You're fantastic, you know! This is unbelievable
that I could be breathing hard as I think of you.
That's some incredible power you possess.
Have you bottled it yet?

I Don't Want to Die
with this Music in Me

I don't want to die with this music in me. The songs that swell each time I speak your name. The tunes that permeate the burning flame. I don't want to die with this music in me.

I feel the need to create this song…a masterpiece of grandiose style. But all the while I drag and pine, waiting for the spark to create the line. Cause I don't want to die with this music in me.

I hear the other songs so well and they all get mixed-up in my head. And when I sit to write this tune…with voluminous flair I start – then boom – nothing! I don't want to die with this music in me.

So start to play upon my heart where I will receive this divine spark. To make me do a tune for you where hearts will turn and I will too. Cause I don't want to die with this music in me.

So speak my name in my ear and make me sing until I hear That one, divine, inspired word I need to make me do this worthy deed. Cause I don't want to die with this music in me.

My Song

My song is one that has been sung many times
before, but because it's my song, I've got to sing
it. I'm in love with a beautiful guy! Yes! I could
shout it to the rafters, but I'll keep it in my heart.
And if you venture to hear these few words, then
you'll know my secret, too!

I thought I would be able to remain less vocal
about this guy, but my joy is spilling over. I had,
for a while, contemplated a mundane existence,
sharing my world with my family and those
friends whose relational ties can venture to the
state of love and care. But not the kind that
makes me sing of times together
--- just him and me –
we---laughing and playing and making love
and laughing some more.

Yes, my song has been sung by many others many
times before, but my song is so special,
I needed to share it, and my wish is
for you a similar song

Separation

The surest sign of my love is that
I respect your freedom.
I therefore set you free and if you don't return,
I'll treasure our moments of togetherness

Today, I Watched My Love

Today I watched my love walk down the corridor
with another. We paused, and glanced – a parting
sigh I emitted as I continued to walk as if this love
had not I ever seen today. My heart felt aches as I
remembered a time where I would have walked as
she – proud to be in the basking glow of the smile
that once watched as we passionately drank of
each other and bathed in the after thoughts of
raptured times afore.

Today I watched my love walk down the corridor
with another. As we paused, my eyes told him I
knew what it was. I saw cordial greetings
transpire, but I, I could not remember her name
because the name was of no importance. As I
took several steps towards the door, I abruptly
turned to see one last glimpse of my love. But
luckily for my heart, they had vanished.

So, I pour onto this paper my thoughts as I reminisce of those times when my love and I danced and I remember the glances of our first meeting when eyes followed me and I felt the presence of a spirit more powerful than my own, whose spirit I wished to know.

I now know that these times shall be locked in the annals of my mind. I pray that I shall in future days look fondly on the good and not remember that one last time.

Today I watched my love walk down the corridor with another. I also watched my heart tear as if tearing was a way it knew too well. I thought I had protected my little heart from times like this, but it appears my vulnerability resurfaced to dissolve any facades of professionalism and coolness towards those things
that allow me to love.

And as I watched my love walk down the corridor with another, I mentally blew a kiss farewell to this love and tried to remember that time heals all.

I Waited For You

I waited for you the other night. For a long time I
watched and stared at the door. But you were not
there. I sat and ate a bite, hoping you would
come…but low, you didn't.
But I waited for you the other night.

Seems as though it's become a habit. You're not
mine – I dare not grab at the fleeting moments
that appear so sweet. But they're not mine and it
would be defeat to dare and dream that day would
come when I wouldn't have to wait
and have such fun.

So I'll go along my merry way
and reflecton this another day.
For the time will come when waits won't be.
For you see…there'll be none of me for thee.

The Me I See In Thee

Bubbling reflections – sideward rejections. Making
me mirror me. As my mind wanders – it does
ponder the many thoughts of thee.

Bright in the revelry of the crevices of my mind, I
process the happenings of the times of you and
me. When I think – I come to know that
before I could love you, I have to love me.
So on these reflections and sideward rejections,
my mirror sees only me.

For only by me can I see thee.
And what I see in thee is in me, you understand?
Come to know me is a process that involves thee.
Through thee, I see me.
Bubbling reflections – sideward rejections. I don't
wish to see. But those rejections are only
reflections of the me I see in thee.

Elusive Butterfly

Love is likened unto the elusive butterfly. When
you think you've got it within your grasp, it
suddenly darts from your fingertips
and flutters about.

As you try to recapture it, the chase becomes so
frantic. In one last stab of final flurry, you move
to catch the butterfly.
It laughs as it dashes out of sight.

After a while, when you have resigned yourself to
the moment of reflection on the elusive butterfly,
you feel a flutter around your ear. You gently
move your hand and that movement indicates
you're not trying to capture. So the butterfly lights
around your face and in your heart.

Do you get the point? Well, the point has been so
hard-hammered, until I had to take time to
commit it to paper. If there's love, set it free.
Don't run to hold on to it. Just enjoy!
If, in the interim, your full intention moves you to
hold on, remember to release. By releasing, you
are going to truly understand. If that love loves
you, it will return. If no return, you can treasure
the time you had to enjoy.

Manifestation

You know the joyful dance of life.
I enjoy dancing with you.
You allow me to snatch
the keys to my liberation.

Sonatina

As my mind took flight on a tune, I devoted a
moment to trip gently on and through the melody
as thought the melody line were you and I was a
string curving around.

Melody unfolds to first movement. I keep up by
bowing slowly and smoothly because I'm sure the
next movement is going to consist of my bowing
getting stronger.

Melody moves from first to second movement.
String anticipates the inevitable, cause here it
comes. Melody becomes stronger and string
courageously bows to keep up. Melody frenetically
trips along as it comes to its climatic state. String
has to pluck to keep up.

Abruptly, melody reaches its high point and
comes meandering down…thanking string for
plucking at its high point and now watching string
curve around.

As melody and string reflect on the moment of the tune, melody decides to do it again, to cement the tune on the mind of the string. So once more melody gives way, but string who has watched melody caste the tune, takes the tune and melody, in turn, devotes itself to the medium string had taken....of curving around.

Melody and string envelope the tune to the point where they cannot differentiate between each other. And as they ebb, they know that the tune will forever play.

The Birth

All thoughts have been flying around through time awaiting a vehicle to become born on earth. One thought has manifested itself and considered me to be its' birthplace. The birth of a thought takes one through pangs of experiences, both good and bad, whose evolution makes for the conjoining of though to vehicle, its' mother.

Realizing this to be so, the thought waits for the precise moment – that of the vehicles pangs of experiences bulging to be delivered. The vehicle bursts with the birthing pangs of resounding thoughts of you! As thought travels through vehicle, vehicle swells and ebbs, trying to release the thought.

Inasmuch as I have been chosen as the vehicle for this thoughts' birth, I must bear the pain of this delivery. For as delivery comes – there are you!

Reflections

I watched the moon tonight and knew that it was also shining on you. A glorious moon peered through clouds expressing its grandeur in like fashion to you. As I watched my pen pass over this paper, trying to capture these fleeting thoughts in words, I find this medium to be lacking because thoughts are more than words…expressions are more than oratories. My total being expresses thoughts of you.

Words, glances, gestures, all are intertwined to make for that totality. And you know! Your every movement, your every gesture, your totality emits more than words could capture.
You know exactly what I need and it comes through more clearly every time.

Of course I watched the moon and gently stroked its rays. I watched the clouds caress it as tenderly as caresses of love. And when I watched the moon, I thought of you!

Somewhere in time I pulled off to stop a while and rest. I rest with such flare it scares me. Resting is supposed to be a time of reflection and replenishing of the body for work.

However, resting to me appears as a brainstorming session as my mind races across memories of not too distant times and not too distant places.

I cross paths in my mind that manifest themselves as triple x-rated and I could never totally express them except in your ear.

Hey! Do you want to hear! Well, lean over and I'll whisper the desires of my heart and make your libido do a somersault. Hey! If I do whisper, don't take me seriously 'cause these are fantasies and if they become reality, then my fantasies will become more bizarre.

Hey! Do you want to hear? Well, come hear, 'cause I feel a need to whisper and allow you to enmesh yourself in my fantasies. If you care to....come with me!

Communing Spirits

I have very expressive thoughts of you as I feel
your presence. Wherever I go, I feel you watching
me. Your spirit is overwhelming and all I have to
do is stop and listen to the vibrations
and you are there.

I don't know how to explain it, but I have this
uncanny sense that you're with me. And even
though the universal law says that no two objects
can occupy the same space at the same time, I beg
to differ with this law, and because I can, I will!

The spiritual force of you tells me differently. You
are in and of me. You opened a new universe to
me and as I move about in the mundane
I never feel it, because my minds' eye is devoted
toward the loftier ideals, the more stately and
serene plateaus that you have expressed
and that I have seen.

I love you for that and more and I shall be
eternally grateful for the revelation – for the
divine scheme revealing such
a beautiful revelation to me – that of you.

Because of our communing spirits, I know that
your presence shall forever be with me. And if
our physical twains never again meet,
our spiritual twains are one.
Think of me sometimes and I'll be there.

In Flight

My mind took flight and landed on your shoulder,
as a butterfly....so light you couldn't feel me there
– but there I was. I wanted so to make you see
me, so I fluttered my wings, but you, so engrossed
in contemplation, didn't see me.

I wanted to tell you that what matters is love,
health, caring, sharing, with the greatest as love,
but my wings could not convey those words.

As you lay to rest, I gently snuggled under your
arm – near your heart – so I could feel the
comfort of your body – its palpitations – its sighs
and movements and with those,
you lulled me to sleep.

In the morning when you arose, my position I
regained, on the broad shoulder. I watched as you
moved through the world you charted and
uncharted, I knew that because God is on your
side, the forces that appeared as devastating
would dissipate through
the resolve of a child of the King.

What comfort this butterfly feels.
What inspiration on the shoulder of a Prince!

Full Service Restoration

I've been embracing the experience of meeting my
soul mate again on this side of the planet. You
know the joyful dance of life
and I enjoy dancing with you.

I've been struggling with the scenario of a foreign
land, foreign people, and learning a process by
which they operate, when the familiar strain of a
melodious, sensual voice hit my ear drum and
allowed me to snatch the key to my liberation
and embrace the experience.

Whatever I was struggling with became secondary
when I realized that you were close enough for me
to smell, taste and absorb.
You have a magnetizing way with yourself and I
find myself again drawn to you….to your
persona….in a different way….a way that friends
as well as lovers embrace after a hiatus –
to rekindle those desires –
to stir the carnal pot –
and reap the benefits again.

Heaven Must Be Like This

I saw a glimpse of heaven and you were there.
Each time I meandered among the clouds,
you were there
Shining and doing those angelic things,
like angels do
At first, you didn't notice me because
you were busy doing the work
But soon you embraced my spirit and
we loved as only we can.
We walked and talked in those heavens
and we shared experiences
And good times and I caught you up
on my goings and comings.
I got so caught up in the reminders of
your spirit, I cried!
I can't remember crying like that in a long time.
I couldn't remember our parting,
but I knew I wished to see you again,
To partake of your spirit.
I think I excited myself too much,
'cause all the emotions welled-up
And I cried tears of joy!

About the Author

Patricia Fointno is a classically trained musician, composer, educator and writer. She was born and raised in Gary, Indiana.

She has earned a Bachelor of Science in Management; and a Master of Arts in Music.

She has a daughter, Erin and two grandchildren, Christian and Kaylie. She currently resides in Arlington, Texas. Patricia enjoys playing piano, writing music, poetry and children's books, meeting people, going to museums, art exhibits and cultural events.

Patricia Fointno has embraced her creativity to produce a poetry book. She enjoys creating music and is always willing to share of her time and talent with others. She hopes to inspire people to delve into their creative spirits.

Patricia Fointno may be contacted for Poetry Readings at: Patriciafointno@gmail.com.

Made in the USA
Monee, IL
07 June 2023

35172612R00031